SHE BECOMES
Unshakable

Rose Parma

She Becomes Unshakable

Written by Rose Parma,
Ministry & Business Breakthrough Coach

Copyright © 2021 Rose Parma

Parma Ministries
www.SheBecomesUnshakable.com
Instagram: @rose_parma_
Email: Hello@RoseParma.com

ISBN: 978-1-7361348-2-5

All Rights Reserved.

Scripture quotations taken from
The Holy Bible, New International Version® NIV®
Copyright © 1973 1978 1984 2011 by Biblica, Inc. ™
Used by permission. All rights reserved worldwide.

Dedication

To all Seven of my Amazing Children — Thank you for loving me and being the very reason I breathe and live! I will forever love you, and be here for you in every season of life.

My Michael — you are Heaven-sent! Your love is patient and kind. You believe in me in a way that I never had. Thank you, Baby, for who you are! I love every bit of you!

To my Mom — Thank you for believing in me. You are a true example of a strong woman. You have a heart of gold.

A gift for you Beautiful...

I have created a gift just for you. Go to ***www.CoachRoseParma.com/FREE*** to grab your FREE Inspiration Cards.

Contents

Broken into Pieces 3
   Scripture to Dive into: 7
   Journal / Prayer / Thoughts: 8

Restoration from the Ground-Up 21
   Scripture to Dive into: 26
   Journal / Prayer / Thoughts: 27

God's Greater Plan- Miracles Happen 41
   Scripture to Dive into: 49
   Journal / Prayer / Thoughts: 50

Navigating the Waters 63
   Scripture to Dive into: 67
   Journal / Prayer / Thoughts: 68

Radical Faith Steps 81
   Scripture to Dive into: 91
   Journal / Prayer / Thoughts: 92

Unshakable 105
    Scripture to Dive into: 111
    Journal / Prayer / Thoughts: 113

Heavenly Vision 127
    Scripture to Dive into: 130
    Journal / Prayer / Thoughts: 131

Additional Scripture to Dive into 145

She Becomes Unshakable Academy 146

Conversion to Living Board 147

Dear Beautiful Woman of God,

The fact that you got your hands on this book is nothing but a miracle. You see, I have prayed for you. You are the woman I wrote this book for. As you dive in, you will hear a story that God turned into a testimony. This is a story of a woman who went from completely broken to Unshakable. In each chapter there is space for you to reflect on your life to journal. You can take notes and get creative. There are even blank pages to draw or color your thoughts. Take the time to pour your heart and feelings out to God. Use the journal space to unravel your thoughts and emotions that are swirling around in your mind. There is healing in the process.

My prayers are that this book will provide breakthrough for you specifically. May God speak to you in a mighty way through the words written in each chapter. May you feel His presence, and peace come over you. This book is meant to be an easy read. It is meant to speak to your heart and your soul. It is meant to open your mind to the greater purpose and calling that God has on YOUR life. God Bless you Sister.

Sending you Love and Hugs,

Rose Parma

Broken into Pieces

From the hospital bed that night, everything changed. My entire world was flipped upside down, and my heart was shattered into a million pieces.

> *As I sit here writing this, the emotions of panic and unbearable pain are flooding through my body.*

Up until that moment, I was a 25-year-old, confident woman, who thought she had it all together. Three beautiful children, married, living in a lovely home that was newly furnished, with the flashy vehicles, boat, and jet ski. I worked part-time running my own business and was attending college to become a registered nurse. Spending time with my family was top priority, and we made it a point to go to church on Sundays.

It was not a life of true ambition or excitement, but it was a life of comfort and consistency. It was the only life I knew since becoming a mom at the young age of 16.

As my aunt stood at the hospital bedside holding my hand, all I could do was sob. Tears were streaming down my face and my heart hurt deeply, more and more with each tear that fell. My ribs were broken, and with every slight movement, excruciating pain shot all throughout my body. My neck was bandaged to stop the bleeding from the knife that was pushed against me, as he threatened to kill me. Flashbacks of being slammed against the concrete floor kept running through my head. It felt like I was in a complete nightmare that at any moment I would wake up from. Remembering the fear in my babies' faces as they tried to save my life, was making me hyperventilate. In that moment of brokenness, emotionally, and physically, I was only worried about how I was going to protect my babies, how I was going to provide financially for them, and show up brave and strong for them.

Not once did it cross my mind "if" I was going to leave my marriage, it was like God was giving me a way out. I knew in my soul that I was never meant to be with this man in the first place. The signs were there all along. I had turned my head for years to the fact that I could have been wrong when I married him.

> *Have you ever done something that you knew was wrong, but you did it anyway, and it turned out to be a disaster? You then kick yourself for not listening to your gut. Welp, that is exactly what happened, and my eyes were wide open. For years, I felt like I was taking one step forward, and then before I knew it, I was taking 3 steps backwards. This was happening in all areas of my life, in*

business, in school, in my marriage, and in my faith. My prayers were often focused on asking God for breakthrough.

My Aunt held my hand tighter and assured me that God would make a way. She began to pray over me, and as she was praying, despite the almost unbearable pain I was experiencing from head to toe, I felt God's peace come over me like a flood. Her powerful words of prayer shifted things for me. It was right then and there on the hospital bed, that I had to make the most important decision of my life.

This decision was about to shift my entire life, for me and for my children. The family they once knew to be, was now different. It was going to be with me as a single mom—I thought this would never happen to me. At that point, I did not really feel like I had a choice. I wanted them to live a life that was in alignment with God's will and God's word. The realization was hard, but you know... sometimes the truth hurts.

This was not a time for me to regret any decisions I had made. It was a time for me to take full ownership of my choices. It was time for me to regroup and collect all the things I learned about strength and honesty, from my parents and mentors in life. It was time for me to get honest with the way I was living. I actually thought I was living a pretty good life up until then, but God showed me different. It was like I instantly was aware of all the sin that I allowed to sneak into my life. All of a sudden, I was very aware of my downfalls that left me in the place of complete brokenness.

You see, this had to happen. God had to break me. This was the answer to my prayers. I had prayed for breakthrough over and over again. God had been giving me signs all along that I was not to be married to this man. I was living a life of my desire and not of God's desire. I was a young teen mom that married a man who was eleven years older than me, who promised me the world. He robbed me from my childhood. He painted this amazing picture that turned out to be a complete nightmare. The enemy works that way. I was young, naive, and pregnant, desperate to create that dream life. God had to make a move for me, because I was not going to do it on my own.

And then, God took what the enemy meant for evil, and He turned it for good.

The ultimate truth in that moment was that I was safe, my kids were safe, and God was going to make a way. God placed it in my heart to reach out to my aunt and uncle that introduced me to Christ when I was a little girl. I asked if it would be possible to rent a room from them in their home for a few months. It just so happened that they had an empty bedroom. This, you see, was a divine appointment. In the next chapter I will explain.

Scripture to Dive into:

Isaiah 61:3

Bestow on them a crown of beauty instead of ashes, the oil of joy instead of mourning, and a garment of praise instead of a spirit of despair. They will be called oaks of righteousness, a planting of the Lord for the display of his splendor.

Proverbs 3:5-6

Trust in the Lord with all your heart and lean not on your own understanding; in all your ways submit to him, and he will make your paths straight.

1 Corinthians 14:33

For God is not a God of disorder but of peace.

Journal / Prayer / Thoughts:

Have you ever prayed for breakthrough, or are currently praying for breakthrough?

Are there things in your life that you feel could be holding you back that are not in alignment with God's word, or His will for your life?

God loves you and you are so important to Him. He wants to bless His daughter. Take a moment to ask God to cleanse you from anything that is not pleasing to Him. Confessing our sins and asking for forgiveness is so powerful. You will feel the weights come off your shoulders.

He will move mountains for you Sister.

Restoration from the Ground-Up

What if this is all on purpose, for a purpose...? All the struggles we go through in life, all the experiences. What if they were all meant to be? Suffering is never fun. Hurt and pain is never fun. I understand this, BUT what if we take a step back and look at all that we have been through, all that we have overcome, through a different lens? I call this, "Looking at our life, and each situation, from a bird's eye view."

When we are in it, it is hard for us to see the big picture. We are often so focused on surviving, and can only hope God will give us the next step. Things cannot happen fast enough for us when we are "in the trenches." Now, from a bird's eye view, the lens is broad, and it is possible to see all the pieces coming together. My life experience that I shared with you in the previous chapter was pretty dramatic and horrific. It very well was the hardest thing I have ever experienced to date. You see, from that experience alone, my life has changed drastically, and today I am here to share a powerful message of hope and faith. I had no clue, in the mist of devastation, that God was writing a new song for my life, and He was preparing me to sing it from the mountaintop.

In the Hurt & Pain—Each day had its own struggles for me to overcome. I will walk you through an in-depth example of a typical week that I experienced. As you read this, you may relate to the rollercoaster ride of emotions, beliefs, and self-talk. On the other hand, you may not relate, because you have never experienced something this devastating, and I pray you never do.

In both cases, I believe God is going to speak to you through this section. It may be for your life, or for the understanding, of what a loved one has experienced.

Saturday Night—I was doing my best to hide the tears from my children. Once they fell asleep, I lost it. My body began to shake, and the tears streamed down my face. As hard as I tried to get it together, the hurt and pain took me over. I felt like my heart was ripping into shreds. Curled in a ball, with my arms wrapped around my knees and my head resting on them, I felt my energy dwindle. I was not even sure how I was breathing anymore. Looking at my innocent, sweet children, sleeping peacefully on the bed next to me, the feelings of guilt and shame flooded over me. How could I let something like this happen to my family...? How could God let this happen!?

My mind was spinning. The tears continued to fall and eventually ran out. There was nothing left inside of me. I carefully crawled into bed to cuddle with my babies, and fell asleep from exhaustion. "God please save us from this nightmare," I prayed.

Sunday Morning—My head was pounding from crying so much. I rushed to the bathroom before my kids saw my puffy eyes, and I put on make up to try to cover it up. My aunt saw through the makeup. She stood in the bathroom doorway and smiled at me peacefully. "I love you. It is going to get easier... little by little. It will take time." Her smile and words brought comfort because I knew she meant it.

> *You see, My Aunt Debbie is the most patient and peaceful human I know. It is a gift that God has blessed her with. This played a huge part in my early healing.*

"I put a radio in your room with a few worship CDs. Listen to them on low volume as you are falling asleep. God will bring peace over you, and you will feel His presence," she whispered. I thanked her and got the kids ready for church.

Worship in church is always so powerful to me. I feel God's presence, and I am instantly reminded that I am safe and fully supported by His love and strength. God reminds me that I am placed where He wants me. He makes it extremely clear that I need to heal and focus on myself as He begins to restore me.

It was like I completely understood what this meant. My children needed me fully present more than ever. In order for me to be the best mom I could be for them, I had to let God do the work in me. This was going to require trust and faith in the Lord and full surrender daily. "Whatever it takes, Lord. Whatever it takes. I surrender," I softly prayed.

Monday-Friday—The weekdays seemed like a blur. One moment I felt like "I got this" kind of attitude, and the next moment I felt completely empty and defeated. As my body began to heal, I was able to go back to work part time. My kids spent a lot of time playing with their cousins and adjusting to our new life. I did all I could to show them how much I loved them and to bring joy into their flipped upside-down world. I prayed over them every morning and every night. The thoughts and emotions they were experiencing must have been extremely hard. All I could do was pray God was restoring us all. Their laughter and smiles were the energy I needed to get through each day. God's love and light shined through them so strong, especially in deep moments of doubt.

As the weeks and months went on...

It did get easier, little by little.

My children and I adjusted, and life as we knew began to shift into a life renewed. Instead of feeling broken, I was flooded with a sense of freedom. It was like God was giving me a second chance to do things right for my children and myself. He was restoring us from the ground-up.

In that season, I quickly discovered the true power of prayer and faith.

Scripture to Dive into:

Psalm 51:10

Create in me a pure heart, O God, and renew a steadfast spirit within me.

Matthew 11:28-30

"Come to me, all you who are weary and burdened, and I will give you rest. Take my yoke upon you and learn from me, for I am gentle and humble in heart, and you will find rest for your souls. For my yoke is easy and my burden is light."

Ephesians 2:8-9

For it is by grace you have been saved, through faith—and this is not from yourselves, it is the gift of God—not by works, so that no one can boast.

Malachi 4:2

But for you who revere my name, the sun of righteousness will rise with healing in its rays. And you will go out and frolic like well-fed calves.

Journal / Prayer / Thoughts:

What are some things you can to bring peace into your life?

How can you expand this list?

Write a letter to God of full surrender. What pain are you holding onto? It is time to lay it at the feet of Jesus so He can begin to RESTORE YOU.

Dear God,

I lay_____ at your feet. (Let it all out... emotionally, physically, mentally, and spiritually.)

God's Greater Plan- Miracles Happen

Understanding that God's plan is far greater than our own plans, is a breath of fresh air. Just think about this for a second. We don't have to have it all figured out. How many times in your life did you find yourself putting together (in great detail) a plan for how the next season will play out, and then the reality hits that God had a different plan. I strongly believe in diving deep into the desires of our hearts, creating a vision, and making it extremely clear.

> *In fact, there are several scriptures in the Bible that speak on this. At the end of this chapter, I will list a few for you to reflect on.*

There is a difference however, in really allowing God to lead our steps, and getting in full alignment with what God is calling us to do.

As I was on a beautiful path to healing, I learned to seek God and His will for my life on a deeper level. There were so many times when I felt like I was doing the best I could, but was struggling to stay above the water. I returned to college and was working part time. My number one focus was to provide the best life I could for my children, and to build a deeper relationship with Jesus, all in the process of self-discovery. My days and nights were continuously busy, and often felt like a mix between calculated and organized chaos. Our days would start as the sun was coming up, and I would study for college into the late hours of the night.

> *When I was in it, I felt like this chaos was never going to end. As I look back, I see that it was an exceedingly small but mighty piece of what God was leading me to.*

The time had come where I finally finished my prerequisites for nursing school. It had taken me seven long years. At that time, there were so many people going to school to become a nurse, that it was extremely challenging to get accepted into any nursing program. That was not going to stop me. I have always had this internal drive and determination to accomplish what I could envision in my mind.

> *I now see this as a gift of being a seer – having the ability to have clear downloads from God that come to me as a vision.*

With each application for nursing school, I attached a prayer of guidance to be accepted into the program that God wanted me to be in, with the people He wanted me to be connected to.

Every week I would check the mail eagerly waiting for an acceptance letter. Time and time again, I would open an envelope, with my heart racing, in hopes that it was the letter I had been waiting for. Time and time again, I was disappointed with a letter of denial. My heart would break, and I was left feeling defeated. "God, I know you have called me to be a nurse. I know the desire you have placed in my heart. Lord, why do I keep getting denied?" I prayed with tears streaming down my face. God spoke so clear to me, "Trust me, my precious daughter. I will not let you down. Keep your faith and trust me."

> *When we are in the middle of our life circumstances, it is hard for us to see the full picture of what God sees. This is when our faith needs to be fully activated. Often, God will present a miracle, big or small, to remind us that He is in full control. God wants us to lean in, listen, and be open to what He is speaking to us.*

He says, *"Be still, and know that I am God; I will be exalted among the nations, I will be exalted in the earth." – Psalm 46:10*

When I was in the waiting period of being accepted into nursing school, God was taking this time to teach me to fully trust that He is in control. I started to experience miracles in every area of my life. I would find envelopes of money that I hid from myself several months prior, and it was the exact dollar amount I needed to pay a bill that was due. My children would say things to me that were direct answers to the prayers I had been asking God to answer. My business was experiencing growth beyond imagination. I was given the opportunity to work as an office manager from home part-time, which was a huge blessing financially. God began to heighten my spiritual gift of visions in a way that I could barely wrap my mind around.

In college, I was also experiencing breakthrough. I was diagnosed with ADD/ADHD. One of my professors noticed my learning style did not fit "inside the box." She referred me to get tested, and several weeks later I was labeled with several "learning disabilities." School did not come easy for me, but I was not letting it stop me. I kept praying and moving forward in the waiting process.

And then it happened, one long year later. The greatest miracle that would shift my entire life in a heavenly sort of way...

I received a phone call that my acceptance letter was received, but due to the delay of notification, I was very short on time, and it did not look like I would be able to make the move in time to start. I was accepted into a college that was out of town, and would require me to relocate and be ready to start the following week. That was only seven days away... It wasn't possible that I would have to find a place to live, transfer my kids' school, and get all my registration complete. How on earth was this going to happen!? It wasn't humanly possible... or was it?

"Lord, if this is your plan, make a way," I prayed as I fell asleep that night.

That is EXACTLY what the Lord did. He made all of the moving pieces come together. It was only by a miracle that I found an apartment down the street from my grandparents, in the same town as the nursing college. Everything went gracefully smooth, from the housing situation, to my children's school, to me getting fully registered, and ready to start that following Monday. I felt like I was living in a complete dream. The Lord heard my prayer, and He made a way that only He could have done.

> *This was the beginning of a new chapter of my life, and for my children to have a fresh start. It was so important to me to keep my past, my past, and not let it determine who I was, or let it own me any longer. I didn't even have to tell anyone about my past. It was a new story that felt amazing already.*
>
> *The delay was on purpose. I knew God had a plan that was on purpose. Two years had passed since being left in a puddle of blood to die. Two years of picking myself up from the ground, and taking steps each day to better my life, for myself, and most importantly, for my children. It was a long season of discovering who I was as a mom and woman. My self-confidence was being rebuilt, and my heart was healing. A fresh start for my children was really important to me. Nothing could have prepared me for what was about to happen. God was moving mountains.*

The biggest piece of the puzzle was revealed on the first day of nursing school. He was sitting in the same orientation class, the man God created just for me, Michael. He came up to talk with me on our class break. Immediately, the first words that came out of my mouth, were sharing ALL that I just experienced in my life, all that I promised myself I would not share nor let determine who I was. Michael's response was so kind, and just simply sweet. He smiled and kept the conversation going as if it was normal.

I just finished telling him that I am a single mom of 3, my ex-husband tried to kill me, and it took me 7 years to get into this nursing program.

I warned that he should stay far away from me because I could ruin his life.

This is what had been programmed in me from my ex-husband. He often would tell me that I was good for nothing, and that no one would love me.

With Michael's response, I just knew... I knew God had me here for this reason... and it scared me big time! He looked right past all the junk I just shared with him. He was interested in me, as a person. He wanted to know who I really was and didn't seem to let my past push him away.

During that initial conversation with Michael, I let my guard down, and for whatever reason, I felt safe to do so.

Later that night, I cried for hours as the feelings of shame and embarrassment flooded over me.

Why on earth did I just blurt all of my junk out on this nice man!? How could I face him again? He must think I am nuts! I was so embarrassed.

The next day, I realized that I had been over-exaggerating the importance of that conversation. Michael greeted me with a smile and invited me to lunch with a small group of his friends. He didn't seem to have lost sleep over my "life drama", so I felt free to go with the flow and to enjoy making new friends.

God placed some of the most amazing people in my world then, people that I could really do life with. They became my very best friends that were truly a gift from heaven. These were friends that quickly became family to me and my children. Little by little, I was learning to let go of the programming of "not being worthy" or "good enough." They taught me that being loved was a valuable gift, and real. God continues to use these special friendships to shine His love through them.

Over the next two years, God revealed to me that Michael was to be my husband. We dated off and on for a period. I tried to run away from the vision of being married, and I would do all I could to sabotage our relationship.

This again, came from a belief I was holding onto of not being worthy of love, and not being good enough to be a wife.

God was not letting up on His vision for what He had for me and my children. Michael was not giving up either. He prayed for me daily, and at one point he had to step away, so that God could deal with me directly. It was in that time (2 months) that God showed me the clear vision of being in unity with the man He created for me. God was teaching me to love and accept the blessing He had for me. He was showing me what it truly meant to be a daughter of a Mighty King.

We went on to finishing nursing school, and then got married. Today we have a beautiful blended family, with seven amazing children.

Full circle moment—Life is all about the unexpected as we live a life that leads us into obedience daily.

Scripture to Dive into:

Habakkuk 2:2

Write the vision, and make it plain on tablets, that he may run who reads it. [See the end of the book, as we go into great detail on this scripture.]

Psalm 37:4

Take delight in the Lord, and He will give you the desires of your heart.

Proverbs 16:9

In their hearts humans plan their course, but the Lord establishes their steps.

Philippians 4:6

Do not be anxious about anything, but in every situation, by prayer and petition, with thanksgiving, present your requests to God.

2 Timothy 1:7

For the Spirit God gave us does not make us timid, but gives us power, love and self-discipline.

Journal / Prayer / Thoughts:

What are some miracles you have experienced?

What does obedience to God's word look like for you?

Is there something that God is calling you to do but you are hesitant due to fear of the unknown, doubt that you may not have what it takes, or not wanting to get uncomfortable?

Navigating the Waters

Stepping into the new and refreshed identity of Rose Parma was not necessarily a smooth transition. Yes, God had miraculously blessed me with such an incredible man that swept me off my feet, however, there were so many times the "old Rose" would creep up and viciously interrogate me.

> *Now, my faith was solid enough to understand that the enemy would do all he could to keep me in the lies of not being good enough or worthy of this life full of blessings.*

I was reminded often of where I came, from and all of the hurtful things my ex-husband would speak over me and do to me. The thoughts would torment me is such a disgusting way. I would get this pitting feeling in my gut that would trigger the emotions and flashbacks all at once. Was I going to be capable of being a loving wife? Would I fail at being a great mom? Could I protect my children from my ex-husband? Would he get out of prison and try to come after me, or try to take my kids from me? I felt like I was living in fear most days. My palms would sweat, and I would feel my heart begin to race out of control. This would often leave me on the brink of having anxiety attacks. It was truly by God's grace that I was even alive. I knew deep down in my soul that God saved my life physically and spiritually. Emotionally, I was having to navigate through the waters of what it truly meant to be a daughter of a mighty king... what it truly meant to be set free.

Conversations in my head would go something like this:

"Rose—Breathe! You are okay. God is with you and will not forsake you. They enemy is a liar! That was the old you, God has made you new."

I had to repeat this several times, over and over again... slowly until my pulse would begin to regulate. I learned to intentionally focus on my breath – being very aware of the depth and sound of each inhale and exhale. Sometimes this would take me back to a state of true self confidence, but not always. There were plenty of times that I was left with mindfulness that full expression of my emotions was required as I continued to heal. God would often remind me that it would be a continuous process of emotional and supernatural healing.

If I felt the tears wanting to come out; instead of holding them back, I allowed myself the space to let it out. I locked myself in the bathroom or closet so my kids and Michael didn't see me lose my personal power. The tears would flow as my body would tremble with deep rooted emotions of heartache and terror, leading to the feelings of unworthiness. I would let the tears fall until there was nothing left. Every ounce of energy was sucked out of me, and I would feel exhausted. After resting a bit, my mind felt refreshed, and the heaviness was lifted. This entire process would take me back to feeling the confidence of knowing God was with me, and that His plans were far greater for my life, than I could even begin to wrap my mind around.

As much as I tried to hide these emotional waves of breakdown, my husband and kids always knew. They could sense the shift of my energy.

> *The greatest realization was that during my emotional breakdowns, I was never losing my personal power; these breakdowns were, and still are, required for me to fully step into my inner strength. Releasing what is no longer serving me, (emotionally, spiritually, mentally, and physically) is a beautiful part of the healing process and it feels incredibly good once it is out.*

My Michael does an amazing job at loving me and caring for me full heartedly. Each day our relationship is strengthened and our love for one another is so evident. He understands my past and provides the space physically and energetically for me to heal at each stage.

Being a Mama of seven children is always going to require a new level of confidence in who I am as a mom and how I desire to parent. With each child, it has looked different for me, and I have learned to apologize and forgive myself often.

With each new sunrise, there is a fresh start that holds a beat to our new song.

Recently I found a page in my journal that did a great job expressing some of the inner work I did back then and continue to do today.

> *"I used to wonder how I was going to do this Mama Thing and be the best at it.*
>
> *The thing is... there is No "Being the best" at it. I learn as my children grow. I shift sail as needed.*
>
> *Navigating the waters of being a Mama is not always smooth with flow and ease...*
>
> *It can darn well be choppy & the tides are high then low. The waves of emotions can be big...*
>
> *The one thing and probably (the only thing) I have mastered is loving each one of my children with ALL OF MY HEART & ALL OF MY SOUL.*
>
> *I pray for them daily and I know God has a beautiful calling for each of their lives. This goes for ALL 7 of my Babies.*
>
> *They are what my heart beats for.*
>
> *Each day my focus is to Align my Prayers, Beliefs, and Actions. That is the very best that I can do, and it feels beautiful and healthy."*

Scripture to Dive into:

John 14:12
Very truly I tell you, whoever believes in me will do the works I have been doing, and they will do even greater things than these, because I am going to the Father.

Psalm 40:3
He put a new song in my mouth, a hymn of praise to our God. Many will see and fear the Lord and put their trust in him.

Hebrews 11:7
By faith Noah, when warned about things not yet seen, in holy fear built an ark to save his family. By his faith he condemned the world and became heir of the righteousness that is in keeping with faith.

James 1:22-25
Do not merely listen to the word, and so deceive yourselves. Do what it says. Anyone who listens to the word but does not do what it says is like someone who looks at his face in a mirror and, after looking at himself, goes away and immediately forgets what he looks like. But whoever looks intently into the perfect law that gives freedom, and continues in it—not forgetting what they have heard, but doing it—they will be blessed in what they do.

Journal / Prayer / Thoughts:

What areas in your life are you trying to navigate on your own? How can you walk alongside God in these areas?

Let's take a look at the "perfect" mom/ wife/ daughter/ friend/ leader...

Understanding that we are all far from perfect BUT we have the perfect Heavenly Father, can change our perspective.

What "perfect" standard can you let go of and be happy with "doing and being your best"?

How does it feel knowing that God is "creating a New Song" for you to sing?

Radical Faith Steps

Being able to fully express my emotions and thoughts out on paper has been a beautiful practice that I have used for many years. I don't journal daily, rather, I journal when I feel a need to release tension, excitement, or other deep-rooted emotions. Sometimes this is 2-3 times a week. It always leaves me feeling amazing after I get it out, tears included. As I was flipping back through my journal, I came across this beautiful message that needs to be shared with the world, so I will start here by sharing it with You, Sister. This message is about letting go of labels that have been placed over us. (This includes labels that are related to any area – physical, emotional, mental, or spiritual.) Two labels that I decided to get rid of are: "Victim" and having a list of "Learning Disabilities."

From my Journal:

I didn't always feel this way until I found complete evidence in my life

•• ADD/ ADHD is my Superpower ••

It is my Brilliance.

It is my Inner Genius.

It once was a label that was placed upon me as "something was wrong" with me.

The doctors and other individuals that were trying to be helpful said:

"Here is the diet you should follow."

"Here are the meds you should take."

"Limit over-stimulating situations and environments."

"You will need extra help in school."

"You can be overwhelming to others."

"Your brain thinks WAY TOO FAST."

"You'll grow out of it."

"Don't have high expectations."

The list goes on and on... all with underlying "Labels"

Then, one day the most amazing woman said to me...

"You will be amazing at anything you do! You just put your mind to it. You have hypersensitivity to all things around you. This is such a gift if you use it that way."

This woman was the aide in the "disability program" in college that worked with me on a weekly basis.

What she spoke over me that day, changed my life!

She spoke life into the major gift God has blessed me with.

ADD/ ADHD IS MY BLESSING FROM GOD!

When my eyes were opened to this perspective, I saw life through new lenses.

I had to discover how I learned and retained information best.

I discovered that since my brain moves fast, I enjoy listening to audio on double speed.

I learned that watching movies is like torture for me, unless it is about something that I am truly passionate about.

I can take chaos and make it sweet and harmonious in 10 seconds flat.

I can write an entire book in less than 30 days.

I am a phenomenal mentor/ coach... I understand people and can feel their emotions and energy. (Hypersensitivity)

Strategy comes second nature to me as well as leading from the depths of my heart.

I can rearrange and declutter ALL THE THINGS @ rapid speed!

I can be a Mom of 7, Wife, Life Coach, Ministry Leader, Life-school Teacher, and Entrepreneur – all at the same time!

I can get more stuff done in one day than what most people can do in two weeks.

I can paint, make jewelry, hula dance, write books, create courses, run businesses, mentor, design clothing – my creative flow is next level.

I love and care about others deeply.

Yes...

I can get easily frustrated that the world is constantly going slower than in my own head

but

I have learned to be ok with that.

After all,

This is my gift.

No – ADD/ ADHD is not my disability!

No – ADD/ ADHD is not my sad story.

I reject all negative things ever spoken over me.

Thank God for my beautiful helper in college.

I am here to share that same beautiful message with you if you have been diagnosed with ADD/ ADHD.

If you think you have it

or know someone who does...

I am proclaiming a Life of Blessings upon Blessings over you!

Keep reaching for your heart's desires.

YOU GOT THIS!

Discover how you work best and do life THAT WAY.

Love & Hugs,

Rose Parma

Releasing what is no longer serving you is extremely important. When you do the deep inner work, it is when you can fully step into your personal power.

After practicing as a critical care nurse for eight intense years, something huge began to shift inside me. The deeper my relationship was with God, the more I felt this immense sense of desire for *more* in my life. It was confusing to me, because from the outside looking in, I had all I ever dreamed of and more. My relationship with my husband was a breath of fresh air daily, and I felt his love through his words and actions. I was able to homeschool my children and spend quality time with them. My business was steady, and I was truly enjoying working very minimal hours to keep it consistent.

We spent time traveling as a family, and on Sundays we went to church. We were building beautiful friendships in our community and doing ministry work locally. With all of this, I was still feeling a deep rooted desire for more in my life. I started to question if I was being selfish or greedy? It was this irritating thought that would pop up from time to time, and it seemed to happen at the most random times, like when I was driving to work, taking a shower, and often when I was trying to fall asleep.

Time and time again, I would push the thoughts and feelings down of desiring more in life. After all, I had so many amazing things going on already. The daily routine, the comfort of the known kept me complacent. Something inside of me was telling me this was not healthy. I knew I needed to dive deeper into this desire. The hardest part was not knowing what to do next to discover what I was longing for. Taking the next step was confusing, especially because I had no clue what that next step was.

After a long day at the hospital, I climbed into bed, so excited to sleep. I kept tossing and turning trying to turn off my thoughts. There it was again... that thought of "something is missing." I was so frustrated. I sat up, grabbed my journal, and began to write a letter to God. It was a letter of:

"God please forgive me if I sound greedy or selfish... I have no idea what it is, but there is something missing here. Please show me, Lord, what am I not seeing? Is it a different job? Do you want me to go back to school to advance in my nursing career? Are we supposed to be living somewhere else? Please, Lord, open my eyes to what this missing piece is."

> **Prayer is powerful, especially when you believe in its power, and are open to receiving the message and miracles God has in store for your life.*

Within the next several months, after writing my letter to God and praying for discernment, God began to show me different steps to take. It began in my business. He opened doors to expand my income in ways I could have not done on my own. Along with the financial growth, I was blessed with the opportunities to connect with women around the world, to pray with them and collaborate in business. On a local scale, God was showing me how my business was a beautiful form of ministry and always had been. With that new vision, I was inspired to spend more time connecting with women and really being present to hear their stories. I hosted women's ministry events in my home, paint nights focused on scripture and expressive painting, Bible studies, business training events based on Biblical principle, mother and daughter craft events, to name a few.

God reminded me of many times where I was able to encourage and equip women with the tools to transform their lives by coaching them in business and relationships, all on the foundation of His word. He was putting the pieces together so beautifully to show me that all along. He had been using me as a vessel to bless others.

This was a lot to take in all at once.

My husband and I spent a lot of time in prayer and conversation about how blessed we were. Our business was thriving to the point that I was able to cut back on my hours working in the hospital. That alone was a huge blessing. I was pregnant at the time with baby number six, and wanted to spend more time being fully present with my family and in homeschool (life-school).

As the months went on, I started to experience shifts in my spirit. This time, it was more of a sense of urgency to take action. God was calling me to take a radical step in faith and to fully trust Him. In the middle of the night, at 3:33 am, He woke me up speaking two words to me, *"Confident Women."* I grabbed my phone and wrote it down in my notes. The next morning, I shared this with my husband. I had no idea what God was trying to tell me, but I knew it was big because God only wakes me up at 3:33 am when He has a message for me that is of substantial significance. This goes in alignment with Jeremiah 33:3, *"Call to me and I will answer you and tell you great and unsearchable things you do not know."*

It wasn't until about a month later that He woke me up again at our divine meeting time, 3:33 am. This time, He gave me the missing link. *"Confident women is the model of ministry I am giving you. I will give you each step as you are ready. Be obedient to the steps that I give you, and you will see the blessings unfold."*

That night I didn't fall back to sleep, instead I cried silently as my husband and babies cuddled in bed with me.

I cried because I felt gratitude beyond description. God saw me capable and worthy as a vessel to be used in a mighty way. HE was choosing Me. All that I had been through in my past, all the wrong decisions and mistakes I made in life... God was choosing Me to do work for Him. I was so honored and humbled in that moment.

I was not exactly sure how this was going to work or what each step would entail. All I knew, was that my entire body, my entire heart, and my entire soul was all in. Whatever God was leading me to, He was going to provide the details, and He was going to carry me through.

My prayer that day was,

"Lord, I am ready. What is the next step? I promise to walk in complete obedience."

The Lord answered me, and it was clear as day... He said something I did not expect at all, *"QUIT YOUR NURSING JOB!"*

Scripture to Dive into:

Matthew 17:20

He replied, "Because you have so little faith. Truly I tell you, if you have faith as small as a mustard seed, you can say to this mountain, 'Move from here to there,' and it will move. Nothing will be impossible for you."

Galatians 6:9

Let us not become weary in doing good, for at the proper time we will reap a harvest if we do not give up.

Acts 4:31

After they prayed, the place where they were meeting was shaken. And they were all filled with the Holy Spirit and spoke the word of God boldly.

Journal / Prayer / Thoughts:

God will speak to us in different ways and at different times. It is often when we are alone and in a quiet space that we can hear Him the clearest. (This is why I am woken up at 3:33 am, or I hear from God while I am taking a shower, a walk, or resting.)

Is there a special time when you hear from God?

How can you *Make Time* to connect deeper with our Heavenly Father?

Do you feel complete in life, or is there a part of you that feels like there is more that God has in store for you?

Do you feel a tug to step into that greater calling God has on your life?

What is coming up for you as you are reading this chapter?

Unshakable

"Quit my nursing job!?!"

My head was swirling, and I began to feel quite dizzy. Why on earth did God want me to quit my nursing job? This made no sense AT ALL! Didn't God know it took me 10 years to become a nurse? My family was finally at a point where we were thriving financially and enjoying time together. We were completely comfortable at that point in all areas of our life. To quit my job all together would really cause some shifting that I wasn't sure would go well.

For a week straight, I lifted this idea up to the Lord and voiced my arguments with Him on why this would have not been a good idea. God was so gentle and patient with me as I was working through this.

> *I have the belief that God will answer me in rapid speed. It does not need to take weeks, months, or even years to get a clear answer. I also pray for extreme clarity with no gray area. This is a strong belief—*

*and this is exactly how God shows up for my husband and me, every time. This process is taught in depth in my masterclass **Align.** See end of book for details.*

If you are feeling blocked from hearing from God, go back to the last thing He has told you to do, and keep doing that. The more you spend time in prayer and God's word, the more you will hear from him. It is about building a solid relationship with our Heavenly Father.

God answered me with complete discernment that I was to quit my job, and when I took that step, He would then show me the next step to take. It was really that simple. He reminded me to stay focused *on Proverbs 3:3-7:*

Let love and faithfulness never leave you;

Bind them around your neck, write them on the tablet of your heart. Then you will win favor and a good name in the sight of God and man. Trust in the Lord with all of your heart and lean not on your own understanding;

In all your ways submit to him, and he will make your paths straight. Do not be wise in your own eyes; fear the Lord and shun evil.

That day I spent time reading God's word and focusing on the book of Proverbs. The living word of God was speaking directly to my heart and to my soul. The point came where I had the conversation with my husband. His reaction was shocking...

"Perfect, then you must quit if God is telling you to quit." That day, I put in my letter of resignation.

Over the following year, God continued to lead us with one step at a time. My business and ministry continued to thrive. Michael and I began to look at life a little different. You see, in that season we did a lot of soul searching and dove deep into discovering what our dreams and vision for the future was. We prayed for Heavenly Vision, and took the actions steps that were all aligned to the greater picture. (This detailed process is what is taught in my signature coaching course, **Conversion to Living Board**. You can find this in the *She Becomes Unshakable Academy* section.)

My entire life, God had been showing me how to dream, wrap my mind around a dream, and then covert it into a living experience, where He gets all the glory. Such a beautiful and powerful process that had been proven to be true, time and time again.

Something was different that time though... God was teaching me how to dream BEYOND DREAMS. It was like, what I call, having Heavenly Dreams that required Heavenly Vision. God began to place more women in my life that would pray with me and link arms in agreement for what God was doing.

Community is so beautiful when you can support one another and pray for each other. Mandy, my Pastor, mentor, and beautiful sister in Christ, walked along side me as God gave me this vision of ministry. She continues to push me to my edges and fully focus on God's vision. Heather, my sister in business and ministry, praying together for God-Sized Dreams, and taking courageous steps in faith, even when we can't see the full picture. Sarah, my sweet sister-in-law, who continuously prays with me and sees what God is doing. She encourages me to be bold and lean on God's strength daily.

There are so many women to mention. Each and every one of my coaching clients are such a blessing in my life and to others. Seeing them transform into a butterfly that is spreading her wings to make a difference in the world. There are also so many amazing women that understand the vision of Parma Ministries, women that link arms in our prayer team, and partner to be a blessing to survivors of trafficking and abuse.

God works to put the pieces all together. It starts with one step at a time.

Taking a pause to reflect, what I knew for sure was that God was calling us to a greater purpose. This was far beyond what we could even imagine. I knew God was giving us the steps one at a time, and that He was lighting the path.

Now as you are reading this, you may or may not be married. That is completely irrelevant to the message I am sharing with you. You see,

God is all we truly need. Anything beyond God is an added blessing. God wants to use you in a mighty way AND He wants to bless you! He wants to meet you right where you are... in your brokenness and in your strength. He wants to hold your hand, and show you a way of life that is not of this world. He wants to fill you with His unconditional love and peace. He wants to mend your hurts and heal you from your past. He loves you, and it is a love that surpasses any love you will ever experience from another human. He cares about you so deeply, after all, you are His daughter.

Yes Sis, YOU are a daughter of a Mighty King.

There will be times when you may be uncertain of what the next step is.

You may be wondering what truly Your God-given purpose is.

At times you may feel as if you do not have what it takes to step into what God has called you to do.

When these questions, thoughts, or feelings come up, it is a great indication that you need to spend more time with the Lord. Get in your Bible and start reading. As you open the Bible, pray that God will meet you where you are, and speak to you in a mighty way through the written word. The Bible is called the Living Word, because as you read it, it is like it is reading you too! You may begin to feel God speaking directly to a situation or circumstance you are experiencing in that very moment. God will speak to you through the pages.

Take the time to journal on what God has spoken to you, and write down the Bible verses that speak to your heart. As you are journaling, let all your emotions out. Let all your feelings out. It is a space to forget about the world, and truly focus on You. This is a time for you to fill your Soul-Cup so that you can show up in the world with your best foot forward.

Scripture to Dive into:

Isaiah 61:1

The Spirit of the Sovereign Lord is on me, because the Lord has anointed me to proclaim good news to the poor. He has sent me to bind up the brokenhearted, to proclaim freedom for the captives and release from the darkness for the prisoners...

Psalm 139:14

I praise you because I am fearfully and wonderfully made; Your works are wonderful, I know that full well.

Romans 12:12

Be joyful in hope, patient in affliction, faithful in prayer.

1 Corinthians 13:4-5

Love is patient, love is kind. It does not envy, it does not boast, it is not proud. It does not dishonor others, it is not self-seeking, it is not easily angered, it keeps no record of wrongs.

Proverbs 31:25

She is clothed with strength and dignity; she can laugh at the days to come.

Mark 5:34

He said to her, "Daughter, your faith has healed you. Go in peace and be freed from your suffering."

Romans 11:36

For from him and through him and for him are all things. To him be the glory forever! Amen.

Colossians 3:23-24

Whatever you do, work at it with all your heart, as working for the Lord, not for human masters, since you know that you will receive an inheritance from the Lord as a reward. It is the Lord Christ you are serving.

Ephesians 3:20

Now to him who is able to do immeasurably more than all we ask or imagine, according to his power that is at work within us...

Journal / Prayer / Thoughts:

Here are some questions to answer while you are journaling.

This is a guide that I often use and share with my clients.

- What am I feeling emotionally?
- What is going on physically?
- What am I experiencing spiritually?
- What are the thoughts swirling around in my mind?

The more you dive into God's word, and the more you speak to Him through prayer, conversation, or worship, the more you will see the power in having a relationship with Him. We will dive deeper into this in the next chapter.

Heavenly Vision

Let's take a moment to look at what really matters in life. What is the big picture here? It is not about how successful we can be in our jobs, in our businesses, or how many followers we have on social media. It goes far beyond that. Success is beautiful, and I think that when we have a thriving business or a job that we love, we can then be a vessel to bless others in our joy, or with finances, or through supporting other businesses. That, however, is not the big picture. The big picture is for us to let God's light shine through us. The big picture is to be kind and loving, to lead others to Jesus as we continuously nurture our relationship with the Lord. This can be combined with success as we operate in our gifts and do our work in the world for the Lord.

Being a mentor and leader in Women's Ministry, it is so beautiful to see the hand of God move through many women around the globe. This includes women writing books to share their testimony and giving God all the glory, to entrepreneurs running their business on Biblical principle, to feeding the homeless, to working with survivors of abuse and human sex trafficking. The list goes on, and the creativity is beautiful to witness. For the women I get to come along side in these ministries and businesses, I continue to lift them in prayer. Praying God's blessing and favor for them to operate in overflow financially, spiritually, and physically. I know firsthand how God can release blessings and miracles in all these areas, and it could happen in an instant. When a business or ministry is anointed, you will see the work or God move. It will be a supernatural experience.

If you are in a season of your life where you are wanting to operate in your gifts, and experiencing the supernatural power of God, I encourage you to take the time to specifically pray for God to use you as a vessel and to speak through you. Ask God to show you the greater plan that He has for your life. Surrender your plans to the Lord and ask Him for Heavenly Vision.

Heavenly Father,

We come to you today to give you all the glory. We thank you Lord, for the specific giftings you have blessed us each with. We want to be so obedient to what it is you have called us to do Lord, and operate in the purpose you have placed us on the earth for. Jeremiah 1:5 says, "Before I formed you in the womb I knew you, before you were born, I set you apart; I appointed you as a prophet to the nations." As we step into this new season, let your blessings and anointing fall upon us. May you give us discernment daily, divine strength, and knowledge to fulfill our calling. Where we are lacking, Lord, I pray you fill in the gap.

We receive your heavenly guidance in all areas of our life.

Thank you, Lord. In your mighty name we pray. Amen.

Sister, I am cheering you on in a mighty way. Look within you for that greater purpose that God is calling you to. There is always room for growth. It starts with the desire to do more and be more. This does not need to look like "hustle"; as a matter of fact, I don't even like that word. Stepping into the next version of you will, for sure, require work. You can choose for it to be amazing. You can choose to be in a form of balance known as harmony. When you make the decision of how you want it to be… you then get on the path to take you there. Many times, that can be the challenging part.

If you are desiring guidance and support; you will love the options in the *She Becomes Unshakable Academy* section at the end of this book.

Scripture to Dive into:

Ecclesiastes 11:4-6

Whoever watches the wind will not plant; whoever looks at the clouds will not reap. As you do not know the path of the wind, or how the body is formed in a mother's womb, so you cannot understand the work of God, the Maker of all things.

Sow your seed in the morning, and at evening let your hands not be idle, for you do not know which will succeed, whether this or that, or whether both will do equally well.

Habakkuk 2:2

Write the vision, and make it plain on tablets, that he may run who reads it. [When it is written down and then implemented, those we lead can "run" with it, and we will see it succeed.]

(This verse is mentioned several times in this book. It is a foundational verse God has spoken to me over and over again. It is also the core on my coaching program.)

Journal / Prayer / Thoughts:

What are some miracles you have experienced?

Do you have a seed planted in your heart that God keeps reminding you of?

Are you unsure of your next steps?

What is it that you desire in taking your next steps?

Are you desiring community, accountability, support, or guidance?

If you haven't already done so, go to **www.CoachRoseParma.com/FREE** to grab your FREE Inspiration Cards. They are the perfect reminders to print and post in your home, office, and car.

Additional Scripture to Dive into

John 14:26

But the Advocate, the Holy Spirit, whom the Father will send in my name, will teach you all things and will remind you of everything I have said to you.

Psalm 121:1-2 A song of ascents.

I lift up my eyes to the mountains—where does my help come from? My help comes from the Lord, the Maker of heaven and earth.

Proverbs 24:3-4

By wisdom a house is built, and through understanding it is established; through knowledge its rooms are filled with rare and beautiful treasures.

1 Corinthians 13:11

When I was a child, I talked like a child, I thought like a child, I reasoned like a child. When I became a man, I put the ways of childhood behind me.

She Becomes Unshakable Academy

Are you ready to take that next step?

Are you ready to discover what *"Living a Life Full of Intention"* looks like for you?

She Becomes Unshakable Academy is a beautiful, safe space for you to dive into discovering whom God has called you to be, nurturing your God-given gifts to share with the world.

There are courses, masterminds, memberships, 1:1 coaching experiences, and so much more.

Go to: **www.SheBecomesUnshakable.com** to discover what may be the best start for you. You can utilize the chat box if you have any questions on where to start. I would love to link arms with you and help you in the process of discovery.

You can also email me with any questions or prayer requests: **hello@RoseParma.com**

Conversion to Living Board

Signature Coaching Program

This is for you if you are desiring to discover your God-Given Purpose. You know there is more for you in life, and you are on a search to be the best version of You.

- Self-paced, easy-to-follow modules
- Unblocking your flow of dreaming
- Recognizing self-sabotage patterns and learn how to move through them
- Opening your mind to Dream Bigger and be ready to receive the miracles God has in store for you
- Breaking down the walls of your past and what may be keeping you feeling stuck
- Step-by-step process on creating your Living Board
- Tangible action steps to take daily that will convert your Living Board into a reality
- Breakthrough strategy Coaching Calls and 1:1 audio guided support

Here is what women are saying about Conversion to Living Board and working 1:1 with Rose:

"I am still in awe of how God placed Rose in my life for such a time as this! A chance encounter on social media with her, brought me the refreshing reminders and next step directions I needed for a breakthrough. I loved walking through the Conversion to Living Board course and the one on one coaching experience. I stand in awe of the goodness of God for how that has changed my life. Having her prayers, coaching, and encouragement to help me see and keep believing! Rose is an amazing woman of God and so gifted at what she is called to do."
– *Jacqueline S.*

"My favorite part of the week is when I have my call with my Coach Rose Parma. I have been on a beautiful discovery process of what breakthrough really looks like. Rose has been guiding and supporting me through this process of being able to identify the things that are not working for me in my life. We work through discovering and strengthening my ability to express my feelings/emotions, and how to bring them full circle, as well as map out a plan to overcome my brokenness. She guides me through the process of leveling up and being in complete alignment with what the Lord has called me to do. It all started with taking her Conversion to Living Board course. That is when walls began to crumble, and I could see massive transformation happening. I thank her so much for helping me realize the potential God has placed on my life." – *Robin A.*

"I have been working with Rose for two years now. I started with a free workshop she was holding then signed up to do Conversion to Living Board course. She walked me through the process of healing things that I had been shoving down for years. She taught me strategies to implement that work with my busy and sometimes chaotic life. Every week on our calls, I learn something new that I can implement for each level of breakthrough. She has taught me how to dream again and how to make my dream a reality. Sometimes it happens so fast that I can't even believe it is happening. Rose definitely has a gift of mentoring and guidance. The best part is that she shows me how to implement God's word in every area of my life." – *Tracy F.*

"As an entrepreneur and mom of 3, I was looking for support in discovering what my purpose is. After doing the course, Conversion to Living Board, my dreams began to flow, and I started to see the potential of what my life could be. I started to experience this new confidence and my business began to flourish. Working with Rose has really given me a new hope and desire to be more in life along with how to live intentional. I want my kids to see me shine and fully live out what I teach them. (You can do anything you set your heart on.) I am so grateful to be a client of Rose." – *Samantha N.*

"As a Women's Ministry Leader, I am often putting my needs and desires last. Over the past 8 months working with Rose has allowed me to truly discover what it means to keep my cup overflowing. It starts in the deep roots of who I am. Each week Rose guides me in discovering who I am as a Daughter of a Mighty King. I have learned so much from her that I apply to ministry and in my daily life. I have been able to show up for myself and for others in such a beautiful way that feels good and in alignment with who God has called me to be. I am so excited for what this next year has in store when I get to work with Rose one on one." – *Natalie B.*

She is Inspired.

She is Empowered.

She Takes Action.

She Becomes Unshakable.

Unshakable

Made in the USA
Middletown, DE
09 September 2023